Muting the Megaphone

Stop Telling Stories
and Start Having Conversations

Kate DiLeo

MUTING THE MEGAPHONE
Stop Telling Stories and Start Having Conversations
Kate DiLeo

1st Edition by Oxygen Publishing
2nd Edition by Elite Online Publishing
Editor: Richard Tardiff

ISBN: 978-1-990093-45-6 (Paperback)

CONTENTS

Are you ready to build a brand
that wins more work in only 4 - 6 weeks?

———⚭———

Learn more:
www.BrandTrifecta.com

PRAISES FOR KATE DILEO

"Kate is a dynamo of energy and brand know-how, and you'll love this book if you're looking to grow your business and make a name for yourself. It's all about conversations – the old ways of shouting and broadcasting to as many people as possible just don't work. This is an easy read full of easy-to-follow steps, concrete examples, and tactics to build conversations with your prospects and customers. Loved it!"

—**Dave Meyer,** President of BizzyWeb
Speaker of Grow with Google
HubSpot Certified Trainer

"Read this book to see where successful marketing is headed. Kate's book helped me realize we had gone from a focus on funnels to stories...but it still didn't work. She beautifully illustrated what was missing. Kate shows the need to sit on the same side of the table and have a meaningful conversation that engages the prospect. I believe in a decade this book will be cited as marketers examine why their funnels and copy never connected or converted as promised."

—**Tom Schwab,** Chief Evangelist Officer & Founder of Interview Valet

"This is what it's all about, this sentence right here: "Stories don't compel people to buy, conversations do." I know that to be fact because I've built a multi-seven-figure agency, SEO National, by doing exactly that. I've never spent a dollar on ads. You know how I get leads and sales? Conversations. People convert on the human element, and that's what Kate teaches you in this book."

—**Damon Burton,** President of SEO National

"As a VP of Marketing I'm often asked, "When it comes to storytelling, where do you begin?" For many years I have recommended Donald Miller's book, *Building a Storybrand*. Today, I recommend Kate DiLeo's *Muting the Megaphone*. Telling a story is a foundational skill which bridges all industries, sectors, levels, and ages. *Muting the Megaphone* cuts through the noise to teach you the actionable –"How."

Whether you are a VP of Marketing or a student graduating from high school, this book has something for you. Kate has synthesized this complex topic into a basic framework. It has become my number one gifted title."

—**Jenny Cotie Kangas,** Director, Talent Acquisition, Employer Branding and Awareness at PandoLogic

"Kate is a partner to our cohort of accelerated companies in the early stage in the sports and eSports space. The difference that she's made and the value that she brings to our program relating to this book is astronomical. Everything about this book is what you should be looking at when covering and understanding brand strategy and marketing. This is a fantastic read and an essential one in the industry."

—**Alex Chalmers,** Managing Partner of Stadia Ventures

"I've been a business coach for over 16 years and worked with over 900 clients, with over 250 of those being CEOs or directors of their companies. I've waded through so many sales and marketing books that talk about the power of brand, but Kate's book is just phenomenal because it cuts out all the fluff. I'm shocked by how much she's given away – not just in the step-by-step creation of the brand, but the crucial piece that is usually missing from other business books – how to implement that brand. If you have a business and have question marks around your brand, this is no-brainer read. Your ROI on this book is going to be insane."

—**David Citron,** Founder of
ExpressoCoaching.com
Director at The UK Centre for Leadership

DEDICATION

To my precious daughter, Veronica.

The day you were born was the beginning of my journey to mute the megaphones in my life. May you, my dear one, also learn to bravely silence the irrelevant voices around you, so you may confidently hear and leverage your own.

Love,
Mama

PREFACE

A quote from the 1994 film adaptation of Louisa May Alcott's classic book, *Little Women*, has motivated me for more than 25 years. In a particular scene, Jo March, played by Winona Ryder, finds herself sitting around the fireplace one evening with her friend, Professor Friedrich Bhaer, and his fellow academics. They partake in a lively discussion on the topic of women's right to vote. After Jo succinctly shares her opinion, one of the men in the room states, "You should have been a lawyer, Miss March." To this compliment, Jo simply smiles and replies, "I should have been a great many things, Mister Mayer."

I should have been a great many things.

There is no truer statement for the incomparable Jo March.

It's important to realize what brought Jo to this point in time in the first place. Throughout her upbringing she never entirely belonged. In a family of gentile sisters, she was the misfit, the oddball, the one who was too big and too bold, and the one who ran around with scraped elbows, jagged words, and illustrious dreams. Jo's journey from girlhood into womanhood was nothing short of awkward, strange, and confusing. She knew she wanted more, and she understood that to stay in her current circumstances would be nothing short of suffocating. She had a purpose burgeoning to be lived.

And so, she took a breath and left.

Jo March moved to New York City to pursue her dream of becoming a writer. She lived in a boarding house with no friends or close family, on her own to explore what the city and world at large held for her. She devoted her time to the singular pursuit of putting her ideas on paper, writing passionately and vigorously. She leveraged her wild imagination to create vibrant stories in which her readers could participate, submitting them to publishers across the city. Yet all her manuscripts were rejected; no matter how hard she tried, she was told her writing simply wasn't what people wanted to read. It was only when she used the pen name of a man, and only when she wrote frivolous stories to satisfy her male editors, that her work was published.

Jo wrestled with this harsh reality. It was clear that they didn't accept her perspective unless she bent it to the parameters of what others said was acceptable and right. It was exhausting and defeating for Jo, to be a parrot rather than a songbird.

With the urging of Friedrich Bhaer, she channeled her disappointment into a positive disruption. She finally broke free from the fear of being accepted by the world's standards, and she scrapped the notion of writing what she thought others wanted. She picked up her pen again and wrote. Yet this time she wrote her truth. Jo crafted her pinnacle masterpiece, perfect in every provoking word. And, to her ultimate dismay, or perhaps not, her compelling message was published for the world to experience. And her words still stand today.

Jo March should have perhaps been a great many things.

Yet her victory lay in the courage to silence the pretense and speak, write, and live in authenticity.

*

Like Jo March, I too, should have been a great many things.

My life has been a culmination of many starts, stops, and pivots. I am humbled. I now find myself an accidental brand strategist and quite the accidental author. This book almost didn't happen. I tried hard. I found a publisher. I set clear and realistic deadlines. I developed a thorough outline. I even had a plethora of pages written.

Yet, all of it was sidelined and ultimately scrapped for more than a year when life smacked me upside the head. My plans for written grandeur paused when I hit extreme burnout. From the outside I appeared fine. I was building 40+ brands per year, networking with intention, and working away on numerous initiatives that would surely help me scale my business. However, I wasn't okay. I was far from it.

I was addicted to the entrepreneurial grind. I ultimately suffered because of my passion, tenacity, and fear. My health was plummeting, my relationships were suffering, and I had no clue how to get off the "hustle hamster wheel." On any given day, while sitting in my office, my average resting heart rate was over 100 beats per minute. I suffered from chronic migraines, constant stomach pain, and swelling of the joints across my entire body. I was physically exhausted, emotionally unstable, and completely unforgiving to myself and others. According to one of my physicians, I was not too far from a heart attack. I'm in my mid- thirties! According to another physician, my body was screaming for me to stop. I had ignored its whispers to slow down for more than a decade. I was breaking, and I needed to undergo a major surgery of mind, body, and spirit.

So, I canceled everything. I got off social media, declined practically every networking meeting, and cut my work schedule back to a maximum of 30 hours per week. I put a pause on working with my coaches (The shock! The horror!) and said "no" to every activity outside of spending quality time with loved ones. I changed my eating habits and type of exercise. I slept more in those months than I had in years.

For the first time in my life, I fiercely prioritized myself. I had no other option.

I stopped striving. I started breathing. I stopped talking. I started listening. And I stopped trying to fit into others' stories, and began shaping my narrative in which I wanted to live in freedom.

After months of silence, I began to speak again. I noticed my voice was more steady, confident, and sure. I didn't feel the need to explain myself. I simply spoke, and I allowed room for others to respond. I began to live my life as an active conversation rather than a passive story—I muted the megaphones around me so I could hear and speak my truth.

Suffice it to say, this past year has taught me a lot. I have learned that life is best lived with a great sense of humor, a deep sense of humility, and a sharp sense of gratitude. I have seen that sacrificing my expectations and embracing my fears has allowed me to fully experience hope and joy. And I have borne witness to the profound reality of letting go of "best practices" which has enabled me to embrace what is right for me.

*

I should have been a great many things.

I will forever be drawn to the character of Jo March. She was a woman who gently held her past, present, and future in one hand as she bravely held her pen in the other. She was a disruptor who confidently silenced the "could" and "should" and "would" of who society told her to be. And she was the ultimate change-maker who dared to ask the question, "What wonderful things could surely happen if I stop telling others' truths and start sharing mine?"

Jo March made the ultimate decision not just to live but to thrive.

And so, she wrote.

NON-FOREWORD

This is where I would normally pay a lot of money for someone super important to put their name here and tell you how great this book is. I'm not doing that. Keep reading if you want to build a brand that wins more work.

Kate DiLeo

INTRODUCTION

The Power of Conversations That Convert

Today's digital economy has turned us into bullish broadcasters. We shout as if we hold a megaphone in our hands, blasting a multitude of messages, hoping to catch our prospects' attention— special offers, explainer videos, case studies and white papers, and sales funnels galore.

Equally, we are inundated with messages that yell right back. We find ourselves helpless to the surrounding noise, hoping we could turn down the volume on the cacophony of daily narratives.

We have become deaf and desperate. We somehow fear that if our story isn't shared or heard, no one will see value in who we are or what we're offering.

All this noise is in the name of storytelling.

Storytelling.

We sell it as the quintessential marketing tactic, and companies spend thousands of dollars trying to craft stories they hope will compel their customers to buy.

Storytelling and branding have become synonymous in today's economy. We naively believe that the power of branding lies in the story's power.

However, the problem with storytelling is that it is a one-way monologue. You talk while your audience listens. No matter how compelling you believe your brand story to be, it still doesn't allow your audience to respond or engage. Even if we have the best intentions to make the customer the heart of our story, it is a story we have written about us. And, when we are on the other side of someone telling us their brand story, we wish they would stop spinning prose, get to the point, and take a breath so we can get in a word somewhere.

All this annoyance is in the name of storytelling.

How ignorant and how egotistical.

The solution is simple.

If we want our target audiences to listen, engage, and eventually buy, we must stop telling brand stories and start having brand conversations. Because when you stop telling stories, and start having conversations, you allow your brand to be the path of least resistance to revenue. Brands that engage in genuine conversations have the power to provoke your target audiences to want to come to the table, build the relationship, and ultimately buy.

If you are ready to build a brand that wins more work, and gets the right prospect to the right table, at the right time, then this book is for you.

SECTION 1

Making the Decision

Have you ever received spam email, a phone call or messages through social media trying to sell you something? It is the epitome of megaphone marketing, and it is obnoxious!

Clearly, these messages have no clue who you are or what you need. You wouldn't be inundated with useless information or ridiculous offers if they did. They would deliver a branded message that builds rapport and directly speaks to how they can meaningfully help you. They would compel you to want to have a conversation.

If you want to compel your target audiences to have a conversation with you, and if you desire to "get the right prospects to the right table at the right time," then you must put some stakes in the ground and decide who you are and who you serve.

You cannot be a chameleon and try to be like your competition. That will certainly not differentiate your organization in the marketplace. You must be you, and remember that by confidently owning who you are, you will attract confident buyers who equally own who they are and know what they need.

You are not in the business of convincing. You're in the business of converting.

And it all starts with deciding who you are and who are your target audiences.

CHAPTER 1

Honing the Tone

My mother was a renowned audiologist for over 40 years. As a child, I recall spending time after school in her office, watching her sitting in her booth, adjusting the sound levels on her systems, waiting for patients to raise their hands to signal whether they heard the sound. Sometimes even the slightest change in decibel level would help my mother determine if someone had hearing loss. She was a master of her craft and gave her professional life to improve the lives of her patients.

As I grew older, I noticed that the audiologist I knew to be a genius was also the woman who had a bad case of selective hearing. An audiologist with selective hearing is the definition of irony, and it is quite the definition of my wonderful mother. To this day, it's hilarious to observe how she can hear my father rummaging through the fridge from the other side of the house, but cannot hear a thing as I try to chat with her while she is watching home improvement shows.

I suppose selective hearing can sometimes serve us, but not always. If we don't hear those around us, we can't always hear ourselves.

I wonder how many of us have selective hearing in our own organization? Do we hear our own brand voices? Or have we gone deaf trying to listen to the din of our competitors.

Nobody will listen to us if we won't listen to ourselves. It's time to hone in on who we are as a brand if we want our audiences to know who we are.

✳

In creating a brand message that enables you to stand out from the competition, it is imperative to understand how you show up. Your brand has a personality and tone of voice unique to you. Your brand is as one-of-a-kind, like a fingerprint or a snowflake. What may seem like undetectable nuances between you and those around you are critical attributes to draw out and effectively write your brand.

I always tell my clients that they should write a brand in the right color pen. If you are a blue pen, we can't write in a red pen. When you write your brand, you need to pick your color pen, so the words are vibrant and accurate. Are you blue or red or pink or green or neon yellow? Are you introverted or extroverted, charismatic or subdued, funny or serious? Everything in a brand starts with recognizing how you speak, sound, and show up. Because what you write should sound like you, look like you, and feel like you—whether plastered across your website, deployed in your email, social media, advertising strategies, or integrated into your most savvy elevator pitches.

Bottom line: You must know your personality and tone to hone in on your brand.

I use three key exercises with clients to help them discern what personality traits and tone of voice are authentic for their organizations' brands: Persona identification, personality analysis, and archetypes prioritization. Each exercise requires a matter of minutes and builds on the next to provide a rich and colorful view of how your brand shows up in the world.

Persona Identification

Ask yourself, "If your brand were a person, who would it be?" Seriously—who is your brand?

Your initial reaction may be to list many adjectives, such as "innovative," "approachable," and "smart," or

5

"humorous," or "kind," and "always doing the right thing," etc. However, go beyond the typical list of characteristics to think in terms of a true persona. Who is your brand?

The fastest and most effective way to solve this is to ask, "If your brand were a public figure or a celebrity, who would it be?"

I have written Oprah brands, Ryan Reynolds brands, and even the occasional Brené Brown brand. Everyone knows how Oprah sounds, (cue, "You get a school! You get a school! Everyone gets a school!"). Everyone knows what Ryan Reynolds sounds like (cue the dry, self-deprecating humor that leaves us wanting more). You get the idea.

Tying your brand to a well-known person ensures you accurately grasp how your brand sounds, because tone of voice is the secret for your brand sticking out in a sea of sameness. It is the recipe for writing a hit tune heard over other elevator music in the world of marketing. It is only by "Oprah-fying" your brand, for example, that you ensure you refine and tighten the language of your brand to sound authentically like you.

As you write, document your persona; use it as your litmus test for ensuring your brand sounds accurate.

Because when you write, you may notice that you write very lengthy and corporate- sounding sentences. Stick to your guns in "Ryan Reynolds-ing" your brand. You will find you can easily tighten up your message and stick to a sense of rhythm and humor true to you. Your message becomes more provocative, and it sounds like something you'd say.

Personality Analysis

Once you define your brand persona, expand on it by accurately discerning supporting personality traits for that persona. Your job is to build this persona with more complexity by understanding how your brand shows up in the world.

The following chart lists 13 sets of common traits. Complete the chart by marking an X along the spectrum of each row where you feel your brand is best represented in terms of its personality/ character. For example, if you ask yourself, "Are we more elite or more approachable?" mark an X under the number one if you believe you are very elite, and mark an X under the number five if you feel you are very approachable. Remember, there is no right or wrong answer. You can be decisive and select what feels most authentic to your brand.

Characteristic	1	2	3	4	5	Characteristic
Elite						Approachable
Serious						Playful
Conventional						Rebel
Authoritative						Friendly
Mature						Youthful
Classic						Innovative
Feminine						Masculine
Complex						Simple
Subtle						Bright
Expensive						Economical
Mainstream						Unconventional
Elegant						Casual
Refined						Strong

The sets of characteristics shown may not seem mutually exclusive. For example, you may think your brand is authoritative and friendly. That's okay. This chart is open for interpretation, and it requires rigor to not over-analyze each word. Go with your gut and ask yourself, "How does my brand show up for its customers, partners, and employees?"

Keep in mind that there is a major difference between how you show up as a founder or leader versus how the brand shows up. Stay focused on the brand and put your personality to the side. The exception to this rule is if you are building a personal brand, in which case you genuinely are the brand, and so the characteristics you choose will also reflect your personality.

As you look at your completed personality traits matrix, do you notice the pattern that your plotted X's shows? Compare this pattern against your brand persona. Does this align with being an Oprah brand, for example?

I've never had an organization see a deviation between exercises one and two. They line up every time with beautiful clarity. If you don't see alignment, go back to the top and double-check that your selected persona is spot-on. Further, make sure you are not completing either exercise for yourself, but for the brand.

Finally, ensure you have completed the exercises with a mindset of how your brand authentically shows up today versus how you aspire to be in the future.

Archetypes Prioritization

You have identified your brand's persona and plotted your brand's personality traits. Now it is time to align them with a proven method for assessing brand personality archetypes.

Archetypes have been around for centuries. It didn't become prominent in the modern world until Swiss psychiatrist Carl Jung developed his 12 archetypes. Known as Jungian archetypes, these 12 "personas" in recent years have been leveraged to develop a brand's personality.

The following chart shows the 12 Jungian archetypes marketers use today. As you review the chart, rank the top three archetypes you feel best represent your brand's personality. You can start with a process of elimination, removing the top six or seven that don't "feel" like your brand. Don't fit your brand into one archetype to define its personality. Fitting limits the full view of how your brand shows up. Instead, recognize that your brand has all 12 archetypes present, and understand which archetypes you lead with the most.

Stay focused on selecting archetypes for who your brand is and how it shows up in the world, versus for you personally. You may resonate with certain

Archetype	Drivers: What Excites You and Spurs You On Values: What Ethics You Live and Uphold Goals: What You Ultimately Want to Achieve Fears: What You Truly Detest or Cannot Stand
Explorer	**Drivers:** Live Life on Their Terms; Experience a Full Life **Values:** Bravery; Adventure; Self-Reliance; Discovery **Goals:** Freedom; Independence **Fears:** Small-Mindedness; Constraints of Daily Life
Sage	**Drivers:** Search for the Truth; Explore Life's Mysteries **Values:** Understanding; Intelligence; Education; Expertise **Goals:** Wisdom; Knowledge **Fears:** Deception; Ignorance
Innocent	**Drivers:** Feel Safe and Happy; Uphold Justice & Truth **Values:** Harmony; Wonder; Goodness; Optimism **Goals:** Happiness; Safety **Fears:** Discord; Doing Wrong
Lover	**Drivers:** Be Loved and Appreciated; Follow the Heart **Values:** Beauty; Romance; Connection; Faithfulness **Goals:** Closeness; Intimacy **Fears:** Isolation; Reason
Jester	**Drivers:** Laugh and Have Fun; Entertain and Enjoy Life **Values:** Humor; Charisma; Enthusiasm; Originality **Goals:** Enjoyment; Spontaneity **Fears:** Boredom; Unoriginality
Everyperson	**Drivers:** Be a Welcome Part of the Community; Find Peace **Values:** Authenticity; Realism; Honesty; Respect **Goals:** Belonging; Tranquility **Fears:** Exclusion; Lack of Authenticity
Maverick	**Drivers:** Buck the Status Quo of Life; Happily Break the Rules **Values:** Independence; Rebellion; Audacity; Individuality **Goals:** Revolution; Freedom **Fears:** Conformity; The System
Magician	**Drivers:** Dream and Enchant; Perform the Magical **Values:** Imagination; Possibility; Intention; Belief **Goals:** Transformation; Power **Fears:** Stagnation; Reality
Soldier	**Drivers:** Overcome with Strength; Fight for a Better World **Values:** Courage; Accomplishment; Sacrifice; Redemption **Goals:** Mastery; Redemption **Fears:** Incapability; Fear
Creative	**Drivers:** Realize Great Ideas; Develop the New **Values:** Expression; Vision; Ingenuity; Non-Conformity **Goals:** Imagination; Innovation **Fears:** Mediocrity; Reputation
Ruler	**Drivers:** Take Control of Life; Gain Deep Security **Values:** Authority; Confidence; Respect; Status **Goals:** Prosperity; Control **Fears:** Chaos; Rebellion
Caregiver	**Drivers:** Give Generously; Support, Care and Help Others **Values:** Comfort; Protection; Patience; Empathy **Goals:** Compassion; Service **Fears:** Exploitation; Selfishness

11

archetypes personally, but they may not be an accurate representation of your brand.

I developed this chart after reviewing dozens of variations of the Jungian Archetype model. Each variation has slight nuances; however, the overarching concepts are the same. If you find a different archetype chart that you like best, use it. The method still works, regardless of whether we label the drivers and values of a particular archetype slightly different.

By the way, these newly discovered tools are wonderful in the hands of visual masterminds for helping you portray your tone of voice through color, font, photography, and other design components.

Finally, consider that, "like attracts like." Now that you have identified your authentic brand persona, tone of voice, and personality, you can home in on who your ideal target audiences are. You can confidently find out who are the like-minded buyers who will resonate with your personality and message.

In chapter two, we will dig into how you can define and find those audiences to deliver a brand message that creates compelling conversations.

CHAPTER 2

Refining the Rolodex

My father was a serial entrepreneur and a serial networker. I have vivid childhood memories of being a part of his regular business activities, whether it was helping him sell products at the Minnesota State Fair, organizing files, or traveling with him on the almost-daily post office run.

Frequently, my sister and I would fight to claim the honorary spot of sitting in the front passenger seat while my dad was driving. But we were often banished to the back seat because the front was taken up by a set of thick three-ring binders filled with business cards. As my dad always told us, these were his most important assets: The Rolodex. He took the Rolodex everywhere. So much so, it made a visible indent in the upholstery.

My dad's Rolodex binders were the bane of my childhood existence, and they taught me an important lesson from an early age. My father showed me first-hand that everyone he met was a potential friend, but not everyone was a potential partner or customer. He organized and categorized his binders with extreme precision. They were not only alphabetized and segmented by service and sector; they were organized with the most influential contacts in the front. Even with thousands of business cards, my dad knew who he wanted to reach with a drop of a hat and why. I believe the ability to build and protect one's Rolodex is becoming a lost art, and it is tragic. For it is quite a simple truth that there is power in who you know, and there is power in why you know them in the first place.

How many of us focus on the masses when it comes to networking and prospecting? Do we go after everyone believing anyone can be a customer? Or do we go after the select few we know have the highest probability of buying?

The truth is that not everyone will like us, let alone buy from us. It's time to refine our Rolodexes to strategically focus on people who have the highest probability of having conversations that convert.

✳

Your brand's job is not to speak to everyone in the world. Your brand's job is to get the right prospect to the right table at the right time. The way to do that is to systematically speak to only the target audiences who will deeply resonate with your message. Even though everyone may potentially need what you have to offer, not everyone is going to care. Before you can write your brand, you need to accept this truth and define your target audiences.

I teach clients to niche in, clearly define their target audiences, and consider the 70% rule. To effectively market your organization, you want to create a brand message that resonates with 70% of your buyers. Having a brand speak to 100% of your buyers is impossible. Embrace that 30% of your revenue may come from other audiences to whom you don't directly target with your brand. They will find you versus you trying to find them.

As you consider your branding and marketing efforts, ask if you are trying to attract anyone and everyone? Do you have a bad case of FOMO (fear of missing out) and worry that if you don't speak to everyone, you may miss out on potential revenue? Are you still marketing to audiences who may have at one point in time purchased from you but are no longer coming to the table? Or are you not sure who you should speak to in the first place? Wherever you are, the good news is you can make the firm decision to strategically niche in on the key groups that will ultimately buy from you.

Bottom line: Be audacious with whom you target to build a brand that builds your business.

I leverage three exercises to help my clients deeply understand who they are going after and why: Target audience selection, buyer criteria definition, and heart pain analysis. As in chapter one, these activities are fast and impactful, and together they provide a holistic perspective on who you should market to and why.

Target Audience Selection

Make a list of all the target audiences or personas to whom you feel you should speak. If you have identified more than a handful, it is time to evaluate your list and eliminate those who may not serve you as well. As you review your list, consider which ones:

1. Have purchased in the last six to 12 months
2. Are fun and easy to work with
3. Are most aligned with your company culture
4. Find the highest value in what you offer
5. Refer you to others in their network
6. Are happy repeat or ongoing customers
7. Make fast and sure buying decisions

8. Have a low level of bureaucracy

9. Know they can't solve the problem themselves

10. Are willing to pay to have their pain go away

After reviewing these questions, do you notice if any of your target audiences aren't an ideal fit? Are there some that seem like a good fit? Are there some that don't fully line up with who will be a buyer, and a great buyer at that, for your organization? If so, make a firm decision to cross them off your list and proceed with building a brand that only speaks to those who need to hear from you, because they are key decision-makers when choosing to work with you to have their problem solved. Stick to the list of who definitely needs what you have to offer.

You don't need to serve every size/sector/role, or every type of buyer in the world. You want to build a brand for the ones who are ideal fits for your organization, and who have the highest probability of being happy, well-aligned customers. So, don't try to eliminate groups who are solid buyers or who are critical for making the purchase happen. Simply evaluate your list and remove any that don't serve you. Over time, as you become great at serving your identified and niched target audiences, your brand reputation will grow and your market share will expand. You can then begin to expand your brand to speak to additional target audiences. However, it would be best if you first committed to niching-in.

Buyer Criteria Definition

Once you have narrowed down your list of target audiences, it is time to define what ideal looks like for that audience.

Remember, of all the potential prospects within your identified target audience, not all are a perfect fit or at a point of readiness to buy. You need to create a set of buyer criteria that defines the ideal prospect so you can message and market to the buyer.

For example, your company decides that it will market to mid- sized manufacturers. You have also determined that the COO of this type of organization is the ideal person to whom you need to deliver a strong brand message, as this person may be the key decision-maker or buyer. These criteria provide a decent outline of whom you may wish to target with your brand at a high level. However, you must go deeper. These two criteria alone aren't enough to write your brand.

Imagine entering a Zoom room or a physical room filled with 100 COOs of 100 mid-sized manufacturers. As you scan the crowd and start to chat with the people, how do you know which ones are potential buyers? Do you spot the 10, 20, or 30 whose business cards you need to get because they are the exact definition of the target audience you want to buy from you? How do you identify the ones in the room who have the exact problem you can solve and who are at a point of readiness to pay? The answer is to develop a systematic set of buyer criteria that deeply illustrate what ideal looks like for your target audience. Build a brand that gets the ideal prospect, versus a decent prospect, to the table. This allows you to listen like a doctor for the right symptoms and indicators to ensure you focus on connecting with legitimate prospects, versus trying to connect with everyone.

The following chart shows an example of how I may list out the top buyer criteria I want. Try to complete a blank version of this chart by filling in the top 10 to 20 specifics to define what ideal looks like for each of your target audiences. As you complete the chart for each audience, consider the questions you reviewed earlier in this chapter, as well as the following:

1. Key pain points they are experiencing that your product/ service directly solves

2. Company attributes, such as size, sector, total revenue, or number of employees

3. Culture characteristics, such as level of internal bureaucracy, coachability, or innovation.

Buyer Criteria for Well-Funded and Founder-Led Startups
1. Has no formal marketing team but may have one person who helps in this area
2. Is looking for reputable marketing partners to help them reach their target audiences
3. Knows they don't know what they don't know when it comes to brand messaging
4. Is willing to bring in outside resources to clearly define their brand
5. Can afford a budget of at least $X for a fixed project, or $X per month for ongoing services
6. Founder is the key decision-maker for investing in marketing
7. Leadership team is well-aligned and communicates effectively on important decisions
8. Is used to seeking outside expertise to improve—doesn't think they have it all figured out
9. Can make timely decisions regarding the investment into branding
10. Has a clear roadmap and timeline on when they want to accomplish the work
11. Has a strong sense of who they are & a clear vision on where they want to go
12. Isn't satisfied with the status quo and wants to differentiate themselves in the marketplace
13. Has a product or service offering that is truly unique and solving a real-world problem
14. Leadership is coachable and willing to follow directions on how to improve their brand
15. Leadership team is willing to invest the time to be in the room to complete the project
16. Is tired of traditional branding methods and needs a disruptive or new approach to branding
17. Recognizes that the ability to acquire investors and customers hinges on a strong brand
18. Knows their current brand message is not resonating as well as it should
19. Needs to synthesize their many brand variations into a single, powerful, and clear message
20. Wants a brand they will embody and one that their target audiences will tangibly experience

After completing the chart, do you see a clear picture of the ideal prospect within the identified target audience? Do you see any similarities between the attributes you have listed for your ideal customer and attributes in your own organization? Are there similar values, levels of bureaucracy, decision-making styles, and cultural attributes? Does this ideal version of your target audience think and behave like you do?

As I mentioned in chapter one; like attracts like. If you see some similarities that is good, because it means you will be attracting prospects who will naturally work well with you and find value in what you offer. Branding is not like dating—because opposites rarely attract. To build a brand that creates a compelling conversation with your target audience, and invites the right prospect to the right table at the right time, you need to focus on speaking to well-defined target audiences with more similarities to your brand than not.

This is about choice. You must first choose who you want to attract and be deeply confident in why you want to attract that person in the first place. Choose to stay firm in your decision, to only work with those who have most of the listed buyer criteria. As you are marketing and prospecting, if the prospect doesn't have 75% of the list, it signals they are not an ideal client at this moment. It could be that it's a budgetary issue, an issue of misaligned leadership, or other realities going on behind the scenes. Follow up in the future to see if things have changed. However, if the prospect has less than half of the list of identified buyer criteria, it may signal there might be serious misalignment. There is a high probability that this prospect is not one you should spend a lot of time trying to win over. Instead, it may be wiser to let them go and focus your marketing and sales efforts on those who are well-aligned.

Finally, allow the process of defining buyer criteria to embolden you to systematically market to the ideal customer and not the decent customer. It is about prospecting smarter, not harder, and you will certainly find that the work you put in to creating well-defined target audiences will improve your bottom line. By sticking to this method you will find that more ideal customers will hear your message and want to work with you.

Heart Pain Analysis

Now that you have niched in your target audiences and have clearly defined them with solid lists of buyer criteria, you need to ascertain what you should say to them to provoke them to want to have a conversation with you. The secret to uncovering what needs to be said is to deeply understand their actual problem. Said differently, you need to clarify the bottom-line heart pain you solve for each audience.

At a surface level, we may think we understand what pain we solve for our customers. Still, I have found we often focus on speaking to a customer's surface-level problems versus speaking to the bottom-line heart pain we solve. Your brand must speak to more than the features and benefits you provide. It must strategically hit on the ultimate pain your customer is experiencing and then state how you solve it.

This isn't to say that the numerous features and benefits your product or service provides aren't important. In terms of the hierarchy of what you lead with when creating a brand message, your multitude of features and benefits come further in the conversation—only once you have effectively stated how you solve the customer's deepest-level heart pain.

We will uncover how you can effectively write your brand message to speak to this pain in the coming chapters. A simple form of root cause analysis, called "The Five Why's Exercise," will clarify your customer's bottom-line need based on the bottom- line pain they are experiencing. As the name implies, "The Five Why's Exercise," is the process of asking a strategic question and then subsequently asking "Why?" five more times to ensure that your answers are the root causes and not surface-level causes.

The following chart is an example of how you may complete "The Five Why's Exercise" to identify the bottom-line pain to solve for your target audience. After reviewing the chart, try to complete a blank version for each of your target audiences. To start, ask yourself, "When it comes to the product or service I offer, what is the bottom-line need for my target audience?" Write down your answer in the first field.

Then ask yourself, "Why? Why does this matter, or why does this target audience care about this?" Write your answer in the second field. Then ask "Why?" again. Continue down the path of completing as many open fields as possible until you uncover the bottom-line need for your target audience. This bottom-line need will point to the heart pain you can solve with your products or services.

Bottom-Line Need(s) for Well-Fund and Founder-Led Startups	
1.	They need to build a brand that will create a conversation with their target audiences.
	WHY?
2.	They need to increase the number of qualified prospects coming to the table.
	WHY?
3.	They need acquire more customers to improve company revenue.
	WHY?
4.	They need to have a stronger bottom line that fosters growth.
	WHY?
5.	They need to keep changing the world with their business.
	WHY?

Bottom Line Need (AKA the Heart Pain You Solve):
These founder-led startups want to change the world.
They can't do that if they aren't winning work. They
need the path of least resistance to revenue, which is a
brand that creates a compelling conversation with their
target audiences. Why? So those audiences ultimately
buy from them versus their competition.

Notice how completing this chart flips the possible brand narrative from being about the thing you deliver to the pain you solve. It moves from a product or service level to an emotional level, enabling your prospect to feel deeply understood. By honing in on solving their deep pain, you can shift your brand messaging from simply stating, "Here are the products and services we provide" to one that says, "Here is the deepest heart pain we can solve for you. Oh, by the way, how we happen to do that is through these products or services." This clearly defines the heart pain of your target audiences that points to why they buy.

As you complete the charts for each audience, if you notice that the heart pain you solve is vastly different between one audience and the next, consider writing a layered brand architecture with multiple sets of messaging that speak to how you solve this pain. I unpack this concept toward the end of this book. For now, focus on the bottom-line need and whether there is a clear pattern among all your target audiences.

The next section of this book will explain how to write your brand message.

Final Thoughts on Refining the Rolodex

Remember, you are not in the business of convincing; you are in the business of converting. It is not your brand's job to convince non-qualified leads to buy. It is your brand's job to speak to highly qualified people who already need what you have to offer.

So, if you have been throwing spaghetti at the wall in the hope that something sticks, you now have the opportunity to speak to those who genuinely need to hear from you.

SECTION 2

Building the Brand

You know who you are, and you deeply understand who you are going after and why.

How do you leverage this information to write a brand that isn't a story but a conversation?

How do you create a brand message that simultaneously captures your authentic sense of self, while deeply resonating with the heart pain you solve for your target audiences?

How do you build a brand that wins more work?

The answer is called The Brand Trifecta, a simple yet provocative three-part messaging formula:

- A clear and concise Tagline that says, "This is what I do."

- A powerful Value Proposition Statement that states, "This is how I solve your problem."

- A set of strong Differentiator Statements that articulate, "This is how I am different from the rest."

The Brand Trifecta's order for delivering a brand message ensures that you can provoke your target audiences to want to know more about you each step of the way. In fact, by not deviating from the order of The Brand Trifecta, each component of your brand message will systematically come together to create conversations that convert.

But a brand cannot build itself. So, get your pen. It's time to write with this strategic approach in mind.

CHAPTER 3

Embracing the Questions

A ll my life, I always had to be right. I was on a constant tirade to prove others wrong, to prove my worth by being the first to talk and the one who always needed to have the last word. Perhaps it was because I was insecure and hurting inside. Perhaps it was because I knew no other way. I was guarded, and I refused to be questioned.

My inability to be questioned prevented me from building relationships and getting where I wanted to go. I was so scared of being challenged and afraid of being proven wrong that I created a lonely world in which I was the only one talking, with nobody listening. It took me a long time to realize that questions weren't the enemy. Holding me back was my profound lack of self-love. It was a long road forward, but I finally broke through these barriers in my late 20s where I no longer led from a place of fearful desperation, but from one of joyful invitation.

I believe there is a precious opportunity to live and lead from a place of invitation, instead of from a place of desperation. And I believe the questions we allow into our spheres will give us the answers we so long to know.

When it comes to writing a brand, how often do we also write from a place of desperation instead of invitation? Do we share too much or nothing at all because we have a fear of being challenged or proven wrong? Or do we welcome the questions of our prospects, customers, and partners, with a recognition that their questions are what will lead them down the path of conversion?

Nobody responds to desperation. They do, however, respond to invitations. Therefore, we must learn how to write a brand message conversation that systematically embraces and invites the questions of our target audiences.

Great brands aren't pretentious. They are provocative. They stand on the truth without being arrogant or boastful. They are simply confident, and they own their expertise. They do not inundate people with paragraphs of information. They deliver a series of short but powerful statements that give space for the target audience to respond.

The Brand Trifecta method is built upon the power of provocation because each of the three brand components in this ordered approach are written to provoke your target audiences to want to know more. Whether your Brand Trifecta is emblazoned on the homepage of your website, layered into your various marketing tactics, or said aloud in the Zoom room, the goal is to get to the point in less than 20 seconds so that someone understands what you do, how you solve their problem, and how you're different from the competition. This is what your target audiences want to know, and it is the stuff that inspires them to state, "Now that is interesting. I want to have a conversation." This is what creates conversations that convert.

To sum it up, The Brand Trifecta creates a conversation by creating room for your target audience to ask each step of the way, "What do you mean by that?", "Can you tell me more?" or "What's in it for me?"

Bottom Line: Your Brand Trifecta is your organization's con- version engine.

As stated previously, three key components make up the Brand Trifecta: Tagline, Value Proposition Statement, and Differentiator Statements. Let's dig into each one, so you understand how to write your own.

Brand Component #1:

A Tagline That Says, "This Is What I Do."

The secret to crafting a Tagline is to concisely tell your target audience what you do.

When you walk into a networking situation, more often than not, the first thing someone asks is, "What do you do?" When someone lands on your website, the first thing they want to know, as well, is what you do.

Unfortunately, we often jumble it up. The most common situation I see is in response to the simple question of what one does, takes more than 30 seconds to answer, and ends up talking in circles, rather than getting to the point. Whether you have been the perpetrator of such a faux pas or on the receiving end, the entire scenario, unfortunately makes both parties want to get out of the conversation altogether. If your brand starts out mumbling along in a complex story, and it isn't quite getting at the heart of telling your target audiences what you do, not to worry. You can begin to right the ship by reframing your brand with a Tagline that clearly states, "This is what I do."

To begin, I will show you the example of my own Tagline:

Building Brands That Win More Work®

Notice how I get right to the point in stating what I do? I do it in a way that alludes to the promise of what I can do for the reader. It isn't pretentious. It's provocative because I have the expertise and reputation to back it up. In fact, I recently had a prospect get referred over to me. In the first five minutes of our initial conversation, he told me that he had taken one look at my Tagline and knew he wanted to work with me. He stated, "I'm willing to work with you if that's what you can do for me. I want that – a brand that helps me win more work. And I want a Tagline that is as powerful as yours."

So, perhaps provocation isn't the enemy. Maybe it's the answer for developing a Tagline that entices your target audiences to want to work with you. But how do you write a winning Tagline? Besides stating what one does, strong Taglines have specific rules that set them apart from the rest.

- They are concise. Avoid using long run-on sentences and keep language condensed. If it includes a colon or semicolon, it is probably too long.
- They are actionable. Use active language instead of passive language. Get right to the point by using strong verbs, versus using fluffy adjectives.
- They are rhythmic. Write in a tone of voice that is yours. Utilize the personality, humor, and language style of your brand's authentic tone of voice.
- They are memorable. Be your fiercely different self in your language so your target audiences remember you over the competition.
- They are provocative. Skip the marketing gibberish and corporate speak. Write to inspire and excite your target audience to want to know more.

Taglines also have specific structure variations that can be utilized. Following is a chart that shows the most common structure variations and ways I may write my Tagline based on the variations I have described, as well as the keywords and phrases I use throughout my messaging. After reviewing the examples, try to complete a blank version of this chart by writing a variety of options for your Tagline. Review each one in conjunction with the set of ideal Tagline characteristics listed earlier to determine which Tagline structure may be best for your brand.

Structure	Example
Phrase Starting with a Gerund	Building Brands That Win More Work
Phrase Starting with a Verb	Build a Brand That Wins More Work
Phrase Starting with a Noun	Brands That Win More Work
Phrase Starting with an Adjective	Provocative Brands That Win More Work
Two Words. Two Words.	Building Brands. Winning Work.
Word. Word. Word.	Provoke. Connect. Convert.

Now, you may be wondering, what about Taglines of prominent brands that don't speak to what they do? Or what about famous Taglines that more accurately state who the organization is versus stating what they do? Why are these Taglines so powerful and memorable in our culture? The simple answer is—look at the marketing budget. These organizations have tremendous dollars to spend to infiltrate every facet of a consumer's life to create brand loyalty. So, unless you have a large budget for advertising, social media, SEO, email marketing, video production, and many other tactics, I recommend you stick to the Tagline formula presented here. Stop worrying about being catchy and start engaging your target audiences with a Tagline that clearly states what you do. Isn't that what your prospects, customers, and partners want to know, anyway?

You may also be wondering, what is the difference between a Slogan and a Tagline? Simply put, a Slogan is often product-specific or campaign-specific, whereas a Tagline applies to the entire organization. You can create a Slogan to sell a specific offering, but your Tagline better be big and bold enough to encompass the entirety of what you do as an organization. Both can work together, but before you get hung up on creating a multitude of Slogans, start at the top to get to the bottom line as fast as possible, using a Tagline that states what your organization does. Because without a Tagline in place your Slogans will not be anchored in a brand that is memorable, structured, or provocative.

If you are getting stuck writing your Tagline, focus on writing your Value Proposition Statement and Differentiator Statements. Sometimes your Tagline becomes obvious at the end of the brand writing process. Don't allow your Tagline to hold you back in the process of writing your Brand Trifecta. Keep going and circle back to it if need be.

Finally, remember that your Tagline should be provocative. If there is any place where you should own your expertise, it is here! Now is not the time to worry that you'll come across as arrogant. Your Tagline should be so provocative that it entices your target audiences to ask, "What do you mean by that?" Inspire them to want to know how you can solve their problem.

And that is where your Value Proposition Statement comes into play.

Brand Component #2:

A Value Proposition Statement That States, "This Is How I Solve Your Problem."

Imagine you are back in the room, networking with people. You just struck up a conversation with someone and they ask, "What do you do?" You reply with your provocative Tagline. They are intrigued and want to know more. They ask, "What do you mean by that?" You respond with a powerful Value Proposition Statement that articulates, "Well, what I mean by that is, I understand that this is your problem, and here is how I can solve that problem for you."

If your Tagline speaks to the core promise of what you do for your target audiences, then the natural follow up is to tell your target audiences how you can deliver on that promise. The second brand component in your Brand Trifecta, the Value Proposition Statement, pinpoints your target audiences' pain and then states how you will solve that pain.

We often hear the concept of a Value Proposition Statement and muddy the waters by writing long sentences that speak more about us than our audiences. We miss the memo completely: Our target audiences don't care about us. They care about themselves. Suppose your brand message is off the mark because it focuses more on you than on your target audience? In that case, you can turn it around with a Value Proposition Statement that clearly articulates, "This is the problem, and this is how I can solve it."

To begin, I will show you the example of my own Value Proposition Statement:

[Pain Statement] Business is a conversation, not a transaction. Yet many organizations struggle to create conversations that convert.

[Call-to-Action Statement] Clarify your brand message and create compelling common ground with your target audiences so they ultimately buy from you versus the competition.

Notice how my Value Proposition Statement is in fact a combination of two statements:

- The Pain Statement - highlights the problem that my target audiences are experiencing.
- The Call-to-Action Statement - directly speaks to how I solve that problem for my target audiences.

Let's unpack how you find the words to write these statements, and then delve into specific characteristics of how these statements should be written.

First, to determine what you want to say, you need to leverage the language you uncovered when going through the heart pain analysis exercise for each of your target audiences. You should have clearly documented what each audience deeply cares about. As you compare the bottom-line heart pain for each of your target audiences, more than likely you will see a strong pattern emerge as to what problem you solve for all of those target audiences. It is this common pain that you will speak to in your Value Proposition Statement.

Next, recognize that your Value Proposition Statement should pinpoint this pain. In fact, both the Pain Statement and the Call- to-Action Statement should work together to give your target audiences an overwhelming sense that they are deeply understood, and have a practical solution in front of them.

The Pain Statement is meant to hit your target audiences between the eyes. It should be the singular brand statement out of your Brand Trifecta that immediately lets your target audiences know that you deeply understand what they are going through, and you call it out. They should hear or read the Pain Statement and immediately think, "You get me!"

Regarding how a Pain Statement is worded, the rule of thumb is that if you were to insert the phrase, "The reality is…" before it, it should make complete sense. If I were to insert the phrase, "The truth is…" in front of the Pain Statement in my own Value Proposition Statement, it would make perfect sense.

So how then do you follow up telling your target audiences the reality of the situation? You tell them how you will fix their situation. Again, this is where the Call-to-Action Statement comes into play. It should directly tell them what to do to have that pain solved. To be specific, it should allude to how they should work with you to solve their problem.

The Call-to-Action Statement should be a true call-to-action that says, "Do this so you get that." In other words, it should directly tell your target audiences, "Take this action with us so you get this pain solved." As for how a Call-to-Action Statement is specifically worded, the rule of thumb here is that if you were to insert the phrase, "Therefore…" before it, it should make complete sense. If I were to insert the phrase, "Therefore…" in front of the Call-to-Action Statement in my own Value Proposition Statement, it is logical and powerful.

Besides clearly pinpointing the pain that your target audience is experiencing, and how you will subsequently solve that pain, powerful Value Proposition Statements also follow the same rules that apply to your Tagline.

And always remember that your Value Proposition Statement isn't about you. It is about your targeted audiences. Focus on speaking to their pain, instead of using words like "our" or "we," and then say how you will solve that pain. Keep it clear, simple, and impactful.

Brand Component #3:

A Set of Differentiator Statements That Articulate, "This Is How I Am Different From the Rest."

Imagine you are back in the same networking room. By now, one person has asked you, "What do you do?" You have replied with your Tagline. They are curious to know more and ask you, "What do you mean by that?" You respond with your Value Proposition Statement.

They should ultimately be won over by your brand pitch and ready to buy.

Right?

Not yet. Here's why.

Many of us might assume that the person listening to us deliver our Tagline and Value Proposition Statement would be ready for the next step, but that is not the case. The reason has to do with some simple buyer psychology.

Put yourself in the other person's shoes. They're meeting you for the first time and have just learned about you and your organization. They need to make sense of what you're sharing. Without realizing it, they will make a comparison because when the brain takes in new information, it tries to make sense of it by compartmentalizing or aligning it to information it already knows. Their brain has put you in a box, and you may think that the comparison traps you; however, quite the opposite. You want the comparison to happen!

The comparison will help you and not hurt you because it sets the stage to deliver the third and final brand component of your Brand Trifecta: Your Differentiator Statements.

Let's go back to this pivotal moment in the networking room. You delivered your provocative Tagline. The person asked, "What do you mean by that?" You then shared your provocative Value Proposition Statement. As the person tries to make sense of what they just heard, they make the comparison. This is where you will most likely hear a question such as, "So, are you like ABC organization or XYZ competitor?" To which you can confidently reply, "That's a great question. I am actually a little different. Here's how."

This is the moment you have been waiting for. This is where you list off the top ways you are different and better than the competition.

It's amazing how they served you up perfectly, did they not? In fact, this pattern of questioning consistently works. Buyer psychology does not fail to bring your target audience to a point where they want to hear exactly how you are different to ensure they understand what you are telling them.

The reality is that it is quite a common occurrence that we try to rush bringing our target audiences to the point of conversion. We are so eager to share all the features and benefits of our product or service offerings that we neglect to realize that the person isn't ready to hear that information yet! So, we skip from sharing our Value Proposition Statement to delving into unnecessary details that overwhelm the other party.

So, don't worry if your brand message has jumped the gun by moving from sharing how you solve the problem to delving into a ton of details around your offering. You can cut through the noise with Differentiator Statements that clearly delineate, "This is how I am different and better than the rest."

I will show you the example of my own Differentiator Statements:

[Differentiator Set-Up Statements] Everything I do is based on the philosophy that brand is the path of least resistance to revenue. I have helped over 300 companies across more than 25 sectors craft brands that bring more prospects to the table through a proprietary approach that is:

[Differentiator Statements]

- Singular. Many agencies are jacks of all trades but masters of none. I eagerly stay in my lane with all things brand to provide you the best possible outcomes that will improve your business.

- Transparent. Branding is a serious investment. I skip the monthly fees and hidden agendas to provide fixed pricing with a clear scope of work so you can make an informed buying decision.

- Fast. Time is of the essence when it comes to hitting your revenue goals. I am quick and agile, collaboratively partnering with you to refine every piece of your brand in only a few weeks.

- Actionable. Your message means nothing if it isn't heard and seen. I show you how to implement your brand across print, digital, and face-to-face channels so it delivers real results.

- Educational. Knowledge is a powerful tool for growth. I leverage a 20+ page Brand Playbook to teach you the why and how of building your brand as a part of a winning business strategy.

Notice how my Differentiator Statements consists of two sets of statements:

- The Differentiator Set-Up Statements. They set the stage with how I am different by stating a key belief and fact about me.

- The Differentiators. They directly speak to how I am unique by listing out the top reasons why I am the one they should choose to have their problem solved.

Let's go deeper on the specific characteristics of how these statements should be crafted.

First, let's analyze the Differentiator Set-Up Statements. Whether one or two sentences, it doesn't matter. What does matter is that these sentences are your first line of defense in answering your target audience's comparison question of, "So, are you like ABC or XYZ competitor?" These statements do this by outlining a key belief that your target audiences need to know before they care to learn more.

Remember that you have told them what you do and how you solve their problem, but they aren't 100% convinced. Your Differentiator Set-Up Statements break down that potential disbelief by calling out a core belief that you more than likely share with your target audience. Said differently, your Differentiator Set- Up Statements create immediate alignment between you and your target audiences because you share a common understanding around the problem they face.

Once you have established the common belief that will resonate with your target audiences, you must serve up the facts of how you are different and better than the rest. This is where your Differentiator Statements come into play. These are written as a catchphrase that highlights the main point, followed by a supporting sentence explaining the catchphrase. They usually come in sets of three to five and often outline what or who you are, and what or who you are not. Finally, they effectively support your Tagline and Value Proposition Statement.

Besides systematically outlining how you are different and better than the competition, your Differentiator Statements follow the same rules that apply to your Tagline and Value Proposition Statement.

Your Differentiator Statements are not passive or demure. They are bold, confident, and speak to your expertise. You know how you are different and better than the competition, which needs to come through in your brand. Otherwise, your target audiences will be left wondering why they should buy from you versus someone else.

If you discover that some of the unique features and benefits of your product or service offering are what makes your organization different, that is okay. Call them out as key Differentiator Statements. Watch out to not get so far into the weeds of listing out every single feature and benefit of your offering; this will overwhelm your target audiences. Remember that they aren't yet ready to know that layer of detail. They are close but not quite there. Stick with the top ways you are different and recognize that further on in the buyer journey, your target audiences will be ready to know all the other details about what makes you and your offering unique.

The Final and Most Important Piece of the Brand Trifecta: The Point of Conversion

You have heard me say more than once that your brand's purpose is to create conversations that convert. Well, congratulations! You have reached the point of conversion. After telling someone what you do, how you solve their problem, and how you are different, your prospect is finally ready to take the next step. Now, the person asks, "So, how does that work?" or "What does that look like?"

The how/what question is the most important question of the brand messaging journey. You've been waiting for this. You have delivered your Brand Trifecta to your target audience. Upon hearing your entire Brand Trifecta, someone asks you how it works or what it looks like; they have shown you that they are ready to know the details. They want to know the nitty-gritty of how you will deliver on this promise.

On your website, this is where the user will click to go to your products or services page to learn more about your offerings. The user may also watch your explainer video to learn more about the features and benefits that your offering provides. They may even go so far as to fill out a contact form to schedule a demo or click to call you right away. Whatever the click path may be, they are ready to go deeper in the conversation with you.

In the networking room, face to face, the conversation turns when the person starts asking you about your scopes of work, timelines, inclusions, and pricing. Your Brand Trifecta has sold them, and they now want to understand the nuts and bolts of how you can solve their specific problem. They will more than likely share details about their organizational issues in the hopes you can directly address those detailed pain points.

Whether you deliver it digitally or face-to-face, remember that until your target audiences hear your Brand Trifecta, they are not ready to hear about your products or services. Embrace this and stick with the Brand Trifecta formula to bring your target audiences quickly and effectively down the buyer journey to where they do want to know more. Whatever you do, stick with the formula. Do not deviate from always delivering your entire Brand Trifecta in the proper order. If you stick to the formula, you will get the desired outcome of a brand conversation that converts.

Final Thoughts on Writing Your Brand Trifecta

Remember that everything you do when writing your Brand Trifecta is about creating the path of least resistance to revenue with a message that gets the right prospect to the right table at the right time. It isn't about telling a story. It's about having a conversation with your target audiences, so they feel compelled to convert into real prospects.

Your brand's job is to help you sell. Period.

Brand is not whimsical, theoretical, or creative. It is not marketing fluff. It is a tangible, practical, living and breathing thing that is your most powerful weapon in revenue generation.

When used correctly, your Brand Trifecta will become the crux of every marketing and sales strategy leveraged by your organization. If not utilized, you will be throwing darts at a dartboard hoping you hit the mark.

Whether you sit on the sales or marketing side of the organization, it doesn't matter. It's time to become aligned on what your brand says and to whom. It ensures that you work in tandem to create synergistic systems that increase your customer acquisition, create cross-functional efficiencies, and ultimately improve your bottom line.

SECTION 3

Starting the Conversation

You have written the most incredible Brand Trifecta. Now what?

It's time to get it out into the world.

That does not mean shouting at your target audiences hoping they will sit up and listen. Again, that is megaphone marketing, and that is not what strong brands do. Your brand's purpose is to create a compelling conversation with your target audiences so you can get the right prospect to the right table at the right time.

So, you need to understand if and when it is necessary to expand your Brand Trifecta messaging and when, where, and how to implement your brand so that it can be the path of least resistance to revenue.

The conversation begins with you.

CHAPTER 4

Expanding the Brand

I began piano lessons at the age of eight, and from the very start I fell in love with that instrument. My teacher Jim was a professional pianist with an incredible pedigree and reputation. Somehow, my mother had finagled him into teaching me piano. Every Tuesday evening he would come over with his bag full of sheet music, ready to teach me the art of the piano.

For ten years Jim taught me more than playing the piano. He taught me that the piano would speak if I spoke. I remember Jim lightly using his pointer finger to push my torso forward and into the piano to show me how to use my body to play louder and with more vigor. Alternately, he would lean back and whisper, "Now with a gentle spirit," to help me recognize when to be quiet and more delicate on the keys. Eventually I learned how to intrinsically adjust my entire posture and being so that the piano itself responded differently.

The art of the piano is not about playing the notes. It's about recognizing that the piano is a living, breathing thing that should be allowed the space to be what it should be, versus trying to fit it inside the original parameters of what was laid on paper.

How often are we trying to force our brand to fit instead of allowing the brand to breathe?

Do we hold our brands hostage by strict parameters of what is written on paper? Or do we actively listen and respond when our brands tell us they must evolve?

Our brands are living and breathing things that must be given the space to grow when the time is right. We must understand when and how to expand our brands to continue to experience the type of conversations that move us.

Often I am asked, "When and how does it make sense to adjust brand messaging?" Your brand should not be updated unless it is warranted. If it's warranted, make the changes quickly and effectively, without overwriting your brand, or leaving it stagnant.

A common mistake is to continuously revise your brand.

I love my fellow brand enthusiasts, but I always caution them on the excitement of consistently tweaking words, hoping that these adjustments will positively impact customer acquisition. The opposite is true. Too many changes can negatively impact your sales. Every time your target audiences run into your brand they hear or see something different. This doesn't create brand consistency or loyalty—it creates confusion!

Leave it alone unless you have data to support the hypothesis that your Brand Trifecta isn't resonating with your target audiences.

Give it some time. I recommend you try your new Brand Trifecta on the world for at least 90 days.

Below I address some of the most common questions on when and how to expand your brand.

What About Vision Statement, Mission Statement, and Brand Values?

By now, you have recognized how a strong Tagline, Value Proposition Statement, and Differentiator Statements work together to provoke the prospect to want to have a conversation. However, you may be wondering how an organization's vision statement, mission statement, and brand values also fit into the picture of developing a comprehensive brand.

People ultimately buy from people. Your brand should still reflect who your organization is regarding the human side: Who you are, what you believe, and what you seek to accomplish. Your vision, mission, and values come into play. These are the brand statements that humanize your organization. You may have the greatest technology or most innovative service in the world, but if you do not also allow your target audiences to get to know you as people, they may not want to do business with you.

Just as The Brand Trifecta should be present on your website and throughout your marketing materials, so should your Vision Statement, Mission Statement, and Brand Values. However, these statements won't show up on your website's homepage because they aren't direct selling statements like The Brand Trifecta. They should show up on the site's about page where people learn who is behind the promise of solving their problem. Put them in your sales decks, investor pitch decks, company overview documents, and other relevant marketing pieces that talk about your company. Remember, these brand statements come after you deliver your Brand Trifecta.

What About Disparate Audiences, Multiple Offerings, or Marketing to B2B and B2C Channels?

Sometimes a single Brand Trifecta isn't enough. It is quite common that organizations who have a disparate set of target audiences, multiple product offerings, or who have both B2B and B2C sales channels find that writing a single Brand Trifecta doesn't work. The solution to these scenarios is to create a layered brand architecture with multiple Brand Trifectas working together. Let's unpack each situation, so you understand how to augment your brand if necessary.

Disparate Audiences

Disparate Audiences are groups of individuals with unique problems that need to be solved. This is often the case if you are trying to sell into a company whose CEO, CFO, COO, and CMO are all key decision-makers. Each leader may have unique concerns that need to be addressed before buying. This can also be the case when you sell into different sectors. One industry may care more about avoiding risk, while another may care more about speed to market. It is a delicate dance to ensure these seemingly disparate audiences see and hear what they need to know about your brand to make a firm decision.

If this is your reality, then you are correct in assuming that a single Brand Trifecta will not fully serve you because each target audience may have unique problems that need to be solved.

So, how do you address this? The answer is in writing multiple Brand Trifectas that work together. Start with a top-level Brand Trifecta that broadly speaks to all your target audiences. This should live on the homepage of your website. Then, develop supporting Brand Trifectas that can be displayed on unique website pages built to target each audience. This messaging approach ensures that each audience understands what is in it for them and how you solve their unique problems, whether it be for a specific industry, leader in an organization, and so forth.

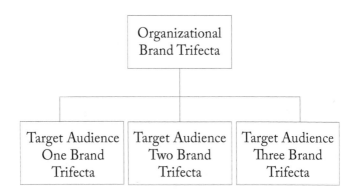

Brand Trifectas within your layered brand architecture will still have the same tone of voice and brand personality, but the content will be nuanced to call out more specifically what you do for each group, how you solve their unique pain, and how you are different from others they may have seen or experienced.

Multiple Product or Service Offerings

Are you selling more than one product or service? In that case, it may be wise to create a layered brand architecture where each offering has its own Brand Trifecta. For example, if one division of your organization provides technology products to startup companies and another delivers technology consulting services for large organizations, then separate branding may be needed. Wherever you find that your product or service offerings serve separate sets of target audiences, supporting and layered messaging are required. If each offering does something different, solves different problems for different target audiences, and has separate competitors, you need a layered brand architecture.

Begin by developing the top-level Brand Trifecta for the organization. Then create unique Brand Trifectas for each product offering. In a situation where each offer has its own set of disparate target audiences, you can take it a step further to create a third layer of Brand Trifectas. Stay the course and develop your layered brand architecture with all of your Brand Trifectas working together top-down and bottom-up.

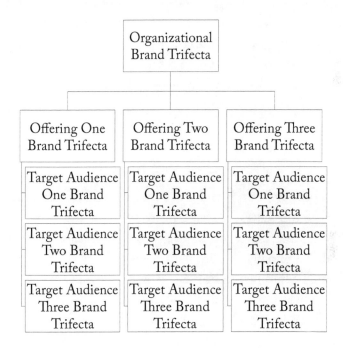

All of your Brand Trifectas within your layered brand architecture should still sound the same but contain different content addressing each group's bottom-line heart pain.

B2B and B2C Channels

B2B is when you are selling products or services to businesses. B2C is when you are selling products or services directly to the consumer. Do you have both B2B and B2C sales channels?

You guessed it. Multiple Brand Trifectas will more likely be at play within your brand architecture. A great example is if your organization has a product you want to sell directly to consumers. Consider state-of-the-art website building technology? Your organization may also want to sell directly to marketing agencies that can white label the technology to deliver better websites to their customers. Both sales channels make logical sense regarding your organization's revenue potential. However, they serve different audiences with different problems and require their own Brand Trifectas.

This situation is the most complex as it requires not only a top- level Brand Trifecta for your organization, but another layer of message for each sales channel, and potentially additional layers of messaging for unique offerings and/or target audiences. It may seem overwhelming at first, but if you do the work on the front- end of developing all messaging you will save a lot of time, money, and headaches. By recognizing that this is the brand architecture you need on the front-end you can streamline the entire branding process, ensuring all layers of messaging work together and create a sense of unity.

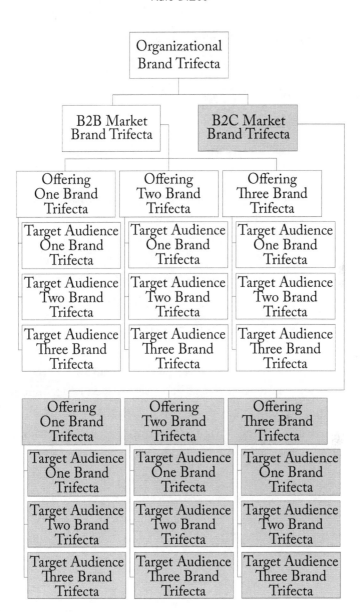

Final Thoughts on Expanding the Brand

Remember that your brand is a living and breathing thing that should evolve as your organization evolves. What serves you today in terms of brand messaging may not serve you in the future. If your target audiences, product offerings, service offerings, or sales channels change, then it is time to revisit your brand.

Chances are you won't need a total rebrand. I have only helped rebrand twice, and that was in a merger situation. Your brand changes won't be a full 180. Instead, they may be more of a quarter turn—slight shifts that ensure your brand speaks to what you now offer, and to whom, in your respective marketplace.

Finally, as I have stated, your brand's purpose is to be the path of least resistance to revenue. If somehow your organization's revenue starts to trend in a negative direction, and if you have already evaluated other pieces of your sales, operations, and marketing strategies, then your brand message may be a component for positively turning the tide. Gather data from your prospects, customers, and partners, and then revise your Brand Trifecta to more effectively speak to what you do, how you solve your target audiences' problems, and how you are different from the competition.

CHAPTER 5

Implementing the Brand

I n my early 20's, I signed up to take salsa dancing lessons. I had always loved the music, was fluent in Spanish after living and traveling abroad, and had a fierce love for dancing after taking dance lessons as a child. These were the signs I needed to assure me that salsa dancing would be a permanent fixture in my life.

I met my instructor, Momchil, while I was out one evening watching a live salsa band. I spotted him across the dance floor and knew I wanted him to teach me. His fluid, relaxed, and confident style was what I wanted to achieve, not the robotic, copycat style I saw many others use on the dance floor. I approached him and said I wanted to work with him, and told him I'd call him the next day to get started. I purchased a pack of 20 private lessons, bought some dance shoes, and dove right in.

I loved every lesson I took with Momchil, and by the end of my time with him I had learned amazing dancing skills and could confidently follow his lead with my eyes closed. I felt like a dance superstar—until the day when I had to leave the classroom and meet up with Momchil to dance at a salsa club.

I took one look around the packed, dark dance floor where hundreds of other accomplished dancers twirled around me, and I froze. Momchil led me through a few songs, but I kept forgetting steps, lost the beat, and eventually I tried to lead him, the poor man! Finally, he stopped me mid-song, grabbed my hands and yelled over the music, "You are dancing like you are practicing! Your lessons didn't teach you steps. They taught you to dance! Trust what you know, let go and just dance!" So, I stopped practicing, and I danced.

When it comes to dancing, the classroom can get in the way of practical applications. Sometimes we become so focused on learning the skills that we seize up and forget them.

How many of us forget to apply our branding prowess in the real world? Do we let our enthusiasm curb our impact? Or do we get out of our own way and do something?

Nothing happens with our brands until we deploy them. It's time to take the training wheels off and experience the power of brands we built to win more work.

✳

Once you have written your brand, you need to implement it swiftly. I can't stress this enough—do not delay getting your brand into the world! I have seen so many organizations write outstanding brands and then drag their feet on taking that brand to market through their various sales and marketing channels.

They then wonder why they do not see a swift financial impact. Clearly, it is impossible to get the right prospect to the right table at the right time if one doesn't even deliver the message. Brands left in boxes go stale and eventually get tossed into the garbage.

Furthermore, the inability to efficiently implement the brand also perpetuates the belief that branding and marketing efforts are simply wasteful and useless overhead costs that don't truly impact the bottom line. What a ridiculous shame. Brand is the path of least resistance to revenue, but only if it is put into the world. So, whether you are in the marketing or sales side of the organization, or perhaps sit in another seat, you have a responsibility to positively impact your company's growth. You need to spearhead the task of getting your brand to market as fast as possible, and with precision.

Later in this chapter you will see an implementation checklist that gives you a great running start for getting your brand into the world. Many of the items in this list can be done without having technical expertise or a marketing agency of record. In fact, many of my clients complete this checklist within the first two weeks of wrapping up a brand project. They recognize this isn't about redesigning their entire visual brand image or building a new website, unless they have strong reasons to do so. This is about swiftly updating written content across all marketing channels so that the brand can begin to create a positive impact on the bottom line. I am not saying a new website or updating your visual brand identity aren't important. I'm saying that those should not get in the way of updating what you already have in place, so that your message doesn't collect dust while you put the finishing touches on those larger initiatives.

So, let's establish some expectations.

A good rule of thumb for implementing your brand is that if you update it because your company colors or logo have changed, it should be updated because your brand message has changed.

The second rule of thumb is to not deviate. Implement your Brand Trifecta across all your channels so that your brand is a clear, consistent message that invites your customers, employees, and partners to have a conversation with you.

Finally, you will notice that many of the items on this list can be done on your own, and others may need the collaboration of other internal or external stakeholders who manage those pieces. If other parties need to be brought in to tackle the work, focus on building a realistic plan on who can tackle what, and when, to get your brand to market as fast as possible.

Stay focused, stay timely, and stay consistent.

The Brand Implementation Checklist:

Highest Priority Items
(Can usually be completed in the first two weeks)

- Website Content
- Social Media Profiles
- Conversation Elevator Pitch
- Presentation Elevator Pitch
- Organizational Bio
- Sales Decks
- Investor Decks
- One-Page Sales Sheets
- Proposals or Formal Statements of Work
- Business Listings
- Email Signatures
- Company Letterhead

Secondary Priority Items
(May take longer than two weeks)

- Brand Style Guides
- Advertising Content
- Email Marketing Content
- Video Content
- Podcast Content
- Search Engine Optimization
- Blogs, E-Books, White Papers, Case Studies
- Online Courses
- Office Signage and Displays
- Swag and Giveaway Items
- Event Signage and Booth Materials
- Job Descriptions
- Employee Handbooks and Onboarding Materials
- Learning Management Systems
- Intranet or SharePoint Platforms
- Partner or Customer Web Portals

Now, let's dig into each item on the list with more specific recommendations on how to optimally deploy your brand message across these channels and tactics.

Highest Priority Items

(Can usually be completed in the first two weeks)

Website Content

Out of all the content you may leverage for your organization, the Brand Trifecta is your most powerful selling language. It should be front and center on the homepage of your website. Before you dig into testimonials, bios on the team, mission and vision statements, and product or service offering content, you need to hit the nail on the head by delivering your Brand Trifecta. To make things easier, I have included a simple wireframe that shows where I recommend you deploy your Brand Trifecta on the homepage of your website.

Please note that I do not mean you should make your website design look exactly like what is represented here. This is a simple representation of the order content and how that should most effectively be positioned on the top-half of your home page. Work this formula into your existing or new website design. Keep the basics in mind for implementing your Brand Trifecta as high as possible on the website homepage to bring the user to the point of conversion, whether to click to go to the products or services page, fill out a form, or click to call you. Whatever your conversion goals may be, the purpose of the Brand Trifecta is to provoke the user to take the next step as quickly as possible. So, do not bury it among your other content. Keep it front and center so that it can do its job.

About Approach	Logo	Services Contact

(Hero Shot: AKA the Main Image)

Tagline

Pain Statement from Your Value Proposition Statement

Call-to-Action Statement from Your Value Proposition Statement

Differentiator Set-Up Statements

(Fold of the Page: AKA Where the User Must Begin to Scroll Down to See More Content)

Differentiators

Differentiator Statement #1

Differentiator Statement #2

Differentiator Statement #3

Services	About	Approach

(Call-to-Action #1) (Call-to-Action #2) (Call-to-Action #3)

(Explainer Video)

Footer

Social Media Profiles

There are many social media platforms, and while I don't list all of them, you can follow the same formula for updating the bios on every platform of your organization.

For platforms with a limited character count, such as Twitter or Instagram, create a shortened version of your Brand Trifecta. I recommend creating a version that is a maximum of 160 characters in either of the following formulas:

- Tagline + Pared Down Value Proposition Statement (Only the Call-to-Action Statement)
- Entire Value Proposition Statement (Pain Statement and the Call-to-Action Statement)

For social media platforms that provide extra space to share about your company, such as LinkedIn and Facebook, you can add your entire Brand Trifecta within the various sections of your company's page or profile. You can also leverage your Brand Trifecta for your personal social media profiles, such as your personal LinkedIn profile, by implementing the following:

- Add your brand's Tagline in the headline section, next to your name and title
- Add your brand's Tagline, Value Proposition Statement, and Differentiator Statements in the Work Experience section next to your company's name

Whether 80 or 800 characters, remember that a strong social media profile should inspire users to want to take the next step with your brand.

Conversation Elevator Pitch

The Conversation Elevator Pitch is what I call a scenario where you show up in the room and deliver your pitch in the course of a natural, back-and-forth conversation. The following is the formula you can use for implementing your Brand Trifecta in a conversation elevator pitch, as well as an example of how I have crafted my own:

- State Who You Are and What You Do
  (Your Name + Tagline)
- State the Problem and How You Solve It
  (Value Proposition Statement)
- State How You Are Different
  (Differentiator Statements)
- State How It Works or What It Looks Like
  (Specific Offerings Details; Features + Benefits)
- State How to Engage with Your Company
  (Next Steps for Getting Started or to Learn More)

Kate DiLeo's Conversation Elevator Pitch Example:

- Prospect: *So, what do you do?*
- Kate: *I build brands that win more work.*
- Prospect: *So, what do you mean by that?*

- Kate: *The truth is that business is a conversation, not a transaction. Yet many organizations struggle to create conversations that convert. I am a brand strategist who helps you clarify your brand message and create compelling, common ground with your target audiences, so they ultimately buy from you versus the competition.*

- Prospect: *So are you like a marketing agency?*

- Kate: *Actually, I'm a little different. Everything I do is based on the philosophy that brand is the path of least resistance to revenue. I have helped over 300 companies across more than 25 sectors craft brands that bring more prospects to the table through a proprietary approach that is:*

  - *Singular. Many agencies are jacks of all trades but masters of none. I eagerly stay in my lane with all things brand to provide the best possible outcomes that will improve your business.*

  - *Transparent. Branding is a serious investment. I skip the monthly fees and hidden agendas to provide fixed pricing with a clear scope of work so you can make an informed buying decision.*

  - *Fast. Time is of the essence when it comes to hitting your revenue goals. I am quick and agile, collaboratively partnering with you to refine every piece of your brand in only a few weeks.*

- ○ *Actionable. Your message means nothing if it isn't heard and seen. I show you how to implement your brand across print, digital, and face-to-face channels so it delivers real results.*

- ○ *Educational. Knowledge is a powerful tool for growth. I leverage a 20+ page Brand Playbook to teach you the why and how of building your brand as a part of a winning business strategy.*

- Prospect: *So how does it work?*

- Kate: *[I then speak to the process of working with the client – my unique approach and service offering]*

- Prospect: *How could I see if this is right for me?*

- Kate: *I'd love to set up a discovery call to learn more about your organization and see if a partnership would be of value.*

Finally, don't let your pitch sit in a folder somewhere. Make it accessible to everyone on your team and do it quickly! I recommend printing copies of this pitch and sending it to everyone in a sales or marketing position, and everyone who interacts with your customers. If you have a remote workforce, don't send it as a PDF. It may go unprinted. Send it to them via snail mail and put it on the desks of everyone in your office. By doing so, you are putting the power of your brand into the hands of every person in your organization, ensuring they can best embody the brand and present it to the world.

Presentation Elevator Pitch

The Presentation Elevator Pitch is the most well-known scenario where you show up in the room and are asked to give your 30-second pitch about yourself and your organization. The following is the formula you can use for implementing your Brand Trifecta in a conversation elevator pitch, as well as an example of how I have crafted my own:

- State Who You Are and What You Do (Your Name + Tagline)
- State the Problem and How You Solve It (Value Proposition Statement)
- State How You Are Different (Differentiator Statements)
- State The Bottom Line of What You Do and How You Help (Repeat Tagline)

Kate DiLeo's Presentation Elevator Pitch Example:

- *My name is Kate DiLeo and I help organizations build brands that win more work.*
- *The truth is that business is a conversation, not a transaction. Yet many organizations struggle to create conversations that convert. I am a brand strategist that helps you clarify your brand message and create compelling, common ground with your target audiences, so they ultimately buy from you versus the competition.*

- *In fact, everything I do is based on the philosophy that brand is the path of least resistance to revenue. I have helped over 300 companies across more than 25 sectors craft brands that bring more prospects to the table through a proprietary approach that is:*

  - *Singular. Many agencies are jacks of all trades but masters of none. I eagerly stay in my lane with all things brand to provide you the best possible outcomes that will improve your business.*

  - *Transparent. Branding is a serious investment. I skip the monthly fees and hidden agendas to provide fixed pricing with a clear scope of work so you can make an informed buying decision.*

  - *Fast. Time is of the essence when it comes to hitting your revenue goals. I am quick and agile, collaboratively partnering with you to refine every piece of your brand in only a few weeks.*

  - *Actionable. Your message means nothing if it isn't heard and seen. I show you how to implement your brand across print, digital, and face-to-face channels so it delivers real results.*

  - *Educational. Knowledge is a powerful tool for growth. I leverage a 20+ page Brand Playbook to teach you the why and how of building your brand as a part of a winning business strategy.*

- *So, whether you are an emerging or established organization, I can help you build a brand that wins more work.*

Remember: Just as I recommend with conversation elevator pitches, print this off and give it to everyone on your team who interacts with your customers, partners, and prospects. Print, laminate, and give it to your workforce (mail it directly to those who work remotely) so they can put this next to their computer and leverage it as key talking points for every phone call, Zoom meeting, and face-to-face interaction.

Organizational Bio

When writing a bio for your organization, the good news is that you can leverage your Brand Trifecta to create a straightforward and robust overview of your organization that invites the reader to connect with you. The formula I use for helping clients write organizational bios is quite simple, with the only nuance being that you end with your Tagline versus starting with it. You immediately capture the reader's attention by speaking to the pain you solve for them. The following is the formula for your organizational bio, and an example of how I have crafted my own:

- State the Problem and How You Solve It (Value Proposition Statement)
- State How You Are Different (Differentiator Statements)
- State The Bottom Line of What You Do and How You Help (Tagline)

Kate DiLeo's Organizational Bio Example:

Business is a conversation, not a transaction. Yet many organizations struggle to create conversations that convert. Kate DiLeo is a brand strategist who helps you clarify your brand message and create compelling, common ground with your target audiences, so they ultimately buy from you versus the competition.

Kate's work is rooted in the philosophy that Brand is the Path of Least Resistance to Revenue®. To date, she has helped over 300 companies across more than 25 sectors craft brands that bring more prospects to the table through a proprietary approach that is:

- *Singular. Many agencies are jacks of all trades but masters of none. Kate eagerly stays in her lane with all things brand to provide you the best possible outcomes that will improve your business.*

- *Transparent. Branding is a serious investment. Kate skips the monthly fees and hidden agendas to provide fixed pricing with a clear scope of work so you can make an informed buying decision.*

- *Fast. Time is of the essence when it comes to hitting your revenue goals. Kate is quick and agile, collaboratively partnering with you to refine every piece of your brand in only a few weeks.*

- *Actionable. Your message means nothing if it isn't heard and seen. Kate shows you how to implement your brand across print, digital, and face-to-face channels to real results.*

- *Educational. Knowledge is a powerful tool for growth. Kate leverages a 20+ page Brand Playbook to teach you the why and how of building your brand as a part of a winning business strategy.*

So, whether you are an emerging or established business, Kate can help you build a brand that wins more work.

A final note on organizational bios: Think strategically about where you need to use this type of paragraph variation of your Brand Trifecta and where the original layout and spacing of your Brand Trifecta may work better. Always anticipate that people do not want to read paragraphs of content and prefer shorter snippets to process. However, there are times and places when a more traditional, paragraph-style bio of your organization is needed.

Sales Decks

If you leverage a slide deck to support your sales process, you want to implement your brand across the first portion of your deck before moving into prospect-specific details. The goal of content organization is to sell first using the Brand Trifecta, and then bring prospects to the point of conversion where they want to know the details to solve their specific pain. Below is a recommended formula for adding your brand message into your sales slide decks:

- **SLIDE 1**: State Who You Are and What You Do (Company Name, Logo, and Tagline)

- **SLIDE 2**: State the Problem You Are Solving (The Pain Statement from Your Value Proposition Statement)

- **SLIDE 3**: State How You Solve the Problem (The Call-to-Action Statement from Your Value Proposition Statement)

- **SLIDE 4**: State How You Are Different (Differentiator Statements)

- **SLIDE 5:** State How It Works or What It Looks Like (Product or Service Features + Benefits; Often Where an Explainer Video Is Utilized)

- **SLIDE 6 AND ONWARD**: Move into the Rest of Your Deck (Specific Offerings or Scope of Work for the Prospect, Next Steps for Engagement)

Focus on keeping things simple. You should not need a sales slide deck that takes more than 15 to 20 minutes to discuss, or one which is more than 10 to 15 slides long. Get to the point quickly with your prospect, so they understand how to take the next logical step.

Investor Decks

Like your sales slide decks, you need to organize your content to hit your brand message first and then move to the other details an investor may want to see. Your goal is to sell the investor as if they were an actual prospect before you dig into financials and additional critical information. I say this because, if you have ever seen the hit show *Shark Tank*, you may notice that when a founder enters the tank, they spend the first few minutes "delivering their pitch" to the sharks before they talk about investment details.

These founders don't walk in and start talking numbers. They first sell the Shark as if the Shark was an actual customer, wowing them with their brand pitch. The investors who are won over will ask more questions about the validity of the investment opportunity. If you are a founder who needs to create a winning investor deck, don't make the mistake of trying to come up with one pitch deck for customers and another for investors. More, don't make the mistake of forgoing your Brand Trifecta altogether and jump right into numbers and details! Stay the course of first delivering your Brand Trifecta before moving to the rest of your deck. Here is a simple formula for incorporating your brand message into your investor decks:

- **SLIDE 1**: State Who You Are and What You Do (Company Name, Logo, and Tagline)
- **SLIDE 2**: State the Problem You Are Solving (The Pain Statement from Your Value Proposition Statement)
- **SLIDE 3**: State How You Solve the Problem (The Call-to-Action Statement from Your Value Proposition Statement)

- **SLIDE 4**: State How You Are Different (Differentiator Statements)

- **SLIDE 5**: State How It Works or What It Looks Like (Product or Service Features + Benefits; Often Where an Explainer Video Is Utilized)

- **SLIDE 6 AND ONWARD**: Move into the Rest of Your Deck (Financials, Market Opportunity, Traction, Key Goals and Timelines, Team Bios, Etc.)

As with sales slide decks, your investor deck should be straight and to the point. No investor is willing to sit through 15 to 20 minutes of introduction slides before getting into the nuts and bolts of whether your opportunity is a viable investment. The faster you deliver your Brand Trifecta, the faster you can wow them and get them ready to talk numbers and next steps.

One-Page Sales Sheets

Whether you leverage a single-page document to provide a high- level overview of your company, or a series of product-specific or service-specific sales sheets, focus on implementing your Brand Trifecta so that your prospect understands who you are, how you solve their problem, and how you're different. Be sure to include the following content in the following order:

- State Who You Are and What You Do (Company Name, Logo, and Tagline)

- State the Problem and How You Solve It (Value Proposition Statement)
- State How You Are Different (Differentiator Statements)
- State How It Works or What It Looks Like (Specific Offerings Details, Features + Benefits)
- State How to Engage with Your Company (Next Steps for Getting Started or to Learn More)

By now, the formula for implementing your brand should be clear. State your Brand Trifecta, and if you have ample room, speak to details on specific product or service offerings, and include a nice call-to-action on how someone can contact you for more information. If you include the information stated in this formula, you have given someone precisely what they need to take the next smart step with you.

Proposals or Formal Statements of Work

Just as with your one-page sales sheets, you will want to incorporate your brand message into your proposal documents or other formal statements of work. Before you list out a scope of work, you should have a page or two that details your Brand Trifecta so that your reader understands what you do, how you solve their problem, and how you're different. From there, you can more fully explain the specific scope of work you plan to provide to the prospect. By incorporating your Brand Trifecta into your formal documents, your prospect, and any other key decision-makers on their team, have all the information they need to make an informed buying decision. Be sure to include the following content in the following order:

- State Who You Are and What You Do (Company Name, Logo, and Tagline)
- State the Problem and How You Solve It (Value Proposition Statement)
- State How You Are Different (Differentiator Statements)
- State the Scope of Work (Specific Offerings Details, Features + Benefits, Timeline, Pricing)
- State the Terms and Conditions (Include All Fine Print)
- State How to Engage with Your Company (Next Steps for Getting Started or Signing on the Line)

As with one-page sales sheets, your goal is to deliver all the necessary information that empowers someone to sign on the dotted line. So, stay hyper-focused on incorporating your Brand Trifecta into the front part of your document before moving into the scope of work and the terms and conditions. You will ensure that every key stakeholder who looks at this document has a clear picture of who you are, what you do, how you can solve their problem, and how you can systematically engage them right there and right now.

Business Listings

As with updating your profiles or bios on social media platforms, you need to update your business listings to include your brand message. Whether to look at reviews or find your contact information, people looking for you online will want to see a glimpse of who you are. You should have your Brand Trifecta front and center on your business listings. Most sites such as Google, Yahoo, Bing, and Yelp offer space for you to add in more than your Tagline. So, my simple recommendation is to include your entire Brand Trifecta: Tagline, Value Proposition Statement, and Differentiator Statements. If there is room, certainly expound and add details about your various product or service offerings, any special offers you may provide, and so forth. However, implement your Brand Trifecta at a minimum so that users clearly understand who you are and how you can help.

Email Signatures

Email signatures are the easiest to do but often the one forgotten. Be sure not to leave your email signature high and dry. Implement your new Tagline into your email signature and don't complicate things— stick with your Tagline and a link to learn more on your website.

Company Letterhead

Most organizations have let go of printing formal letterheads. However, they often have digital letterhead templates like Microsoft Word or Google Docs documents that employees can utilize for writing letters or sending out other important correspondence or documentation. Whatever system you use for your letterhead, update it to include your new Tagline, in the header or footer of the document.

Secondary Priority Items

(May take longer than two weeks)

Brand Style Guides

The Brand Trifecta is your most critical selling language and should be included in your brand style guide. Just as you want to show ways to use or not use your logo, colors, and fonts, you also want to outline your Brand Trifecta and speak to where and how it is utilized. Be sure to include your Tagline, Value Proposition Statement, and Differentiator Statements. Nothing from your Brand Trifecta should be missed in this document. This will be the ultimate handbook on how to move the brand forward.

Advertising Content

Advertising is a complex initiative and an area I highly recommend that you lean on your advertising expert to help you incorporate your Brand Trifecta in the most systematic and balanced way. Weaving your brand throughout your various ads is not as simple as slapping your Tagline across each. This is because each advertising initiative may have a specific focus and purpose. For example, if you are running ads for an upcoming promotion, don't remove critical copy that speaks to the promotional offer because you feel the need to insert your Value Proposition Statement. If there is room and it is logical, consider adding your Tagline into the images of your advertising content. You may also find that your Value Proposition Statement naturally works well as advertising copy for various campaigns. Stay flexible, and work with the experts to systematically think about how you want to best incorporate your Brand Trifecta in and around your advertising content so that it helps versus hinders.

Email Marketing Content

Email marketing is another area where I recommend you lean on your team of experts to ensure they can support you in incorporating your Brand Trifecta into your various campaigns.

Whether you send one email per year or one per day, you will need to weave your Brand Trifecta into your content. Just as with advertising campaigns, weaving your brand throughout your emails isn't as simple as sticking your Tagline somewhere. Each email, or series of emails, may have a specific purpose: Providing relevant, educational content or sharing details on an upcoming promotion. Focus on weaving your Brand Trifecta in and around that content versus overhauling your content altogether. A simple start is to ensure your new Tagline is incorporated in your email's header and footer sections.

You may also find that it makes sense to leverage your Value Proposition Statement or certain Differentiator Statements in the body of your emails. Be curious and open to how you can best infuse your Brand Trifecta into your email marketing content to optimally support your strategy.

Video Content

In today's digital marketplace, organizations leverage video as a powerful way to deliver their brand promise. Video content can range from providing overview information on an organization, explaining how a product or service works, or highlighting specific promotions. Whatever your content strategy, be sure to loop in your video production team to determine how to best incorporate your Brand Trifecta in all your content pieces.

If you have a video that provides a general overview of your organization and its brand promise, it is time to update it to reflect your revised Brand Trifecta. If you have explainer videos that go into more minute details on specific products or services, don't feel the need to overhaul those videos. However, at a minimum, consider incorporating your new Tagline and Value Proposition Statement on your video's intro and outro slides. The same applies to promotion-specific videos. Don't muddy the waters by trying to fit in your entire Brand Trifecta into the short clip. However, if there is room at the beginning or end of the video to show your new Tagline, then do it.

Finally, be sure to update every location where you host your videos, such as on Vimeo or YouTube. Changes don't need to be difficult to ensure these sites best reflect your new Brand Trifecta. If you already include your Tagline in banner graphics or other photos, update that imagery to fit your new Tagline. If you have written a company bio, update it to fit your Brand Trifecta. The goal is to ensure that anyone hitting the page gets an immediate grasp of who you are and what you do, how you can solve their problem, and how you are different from the competition.

Podcast Content

Whether you host your own podcast or are a guest speaker on others' podcasts, you will want to make basic branding updates to your podcasting materials. If you host your own podcast, and if the podcast is directly tied to your organization, then ensure that all channels showcase your Brand Trifecta: Your website, Apple Podcasts, Spotify, iHeartRadio, Stitcher, or Google

Play, as examples. Anywhere your podcast lives should showcase your revised branding. If your podcast is not tied to your organization in any way, or if your podcast topic is entirely unique to you personally, then there may not be a need to update your materials.

Regarding what to update and where, don't worry about incorporating your entire Brand Trifecta; you are working with a limited amount of written space, or only the ability to upload a headshot and a short blurb. At a minimum, incorporate your Tagline into your podcast artwork, or write it into the copy section of your podcasting channel pages.

Finally, the same rule applies to making brand updates if you are a guest on podcasts. Refresh your podcast artwork, as well as your bio, to include pieces of your Brand Trifecta. Remember, if someone has invited you to speak on their podcast about the nature of the work you do, and if it ties to the promise you have outlined in your Brand Trifecta, be sure to update your materials to reflect your brand promise.

Search Engine Optimization

Be aware that any content changes on your website will potentially impact SEO efforts. Search Engine Optimization is an area where I highly recommend you call in the experts. Be sure to notify your SEO team immediately to talk through your Brand Trifecta and proposed changes to your website content based on the revised branding. Looping these experts in early will ensure they can guide you on any recommended changes to your SEO strategy.

Blogs, E-Books, White Papers, and Case Studies

If you already have a strong content strategy in place for publishing blogs, e-books, White Papers, and case studies, don't deviate unless your new Brand Trifecta could have a drastic effect.

If your content strategy is already focused on showcasing your expertise, while providing helpful information that your target audiences can utilize, stick with it. However, suppose you find that your organization has uncovered a drastically different Value Proposition Statement, or a set of new Differentiator Statements. In that case, if none are in your current content strategy, it may be time for an update. Consider adjusting the topic areas for your content to include blogs or case studies that speak to each of your newly defined Differentiator Statements. Consider entire White Papers or an e-book that speaks to your overarching Value Proposition Statement.

Finally, if your content already reflects your revised Brand Trifecta, then stay the course. Double-check that each content piece, and your content strategy, systematically speak to what you do, how you can solve your customer's problem, and how you are different from the competition. At a bare minimum, ensure your new Tagline is emblazoned across any downloadable documents, such as e-books and White Papers, to ensure brand consistency across printed and digital content.

Online Courses

Good news. You do not have to completely change the content in your self-paced or guided courses to include your Brand Trifecta. I always tell clients who offer courses that they don't need to overcomplicate things. Instead, start by ensuring your new Tagline is incorporated into all headers and footers. You can also insert your Tagline onto a main dashboard or landing page that your customers regularly see as a simple way to reinforce your brand message. If there is space and if you feel it is warranted, you can certainly incorporate your Value Proposition Statement and Differentiator Statements onto the main dashboard of your course. You can also update any downloadable documents to include your updated Tagline to ensure brand cohesion between printed and digital materials of your course.

I strongly recommend that you don't worry so much about implementing your entire Brand Trifecta if it will overshadow the actual purpose of the course. Be consistent by having components of your Brand Trifecta infused throughout, while still allowing your course to be the powerful tool that it was created to be.

Office Signage and Displays

Although the world is working remotely, organizations still have office space. If you gather in a physical location, don't miss out on a key opportunity to put your Brand Trifecta in front of your employees, customers, and partners. People need to see and experience your brand for it to be real. Don't make the mistake of allowing your brand to only live online. Put it in the physical world so that people remember your message.

The good news is that it doesn't have to cost a lot to make simple enhancements that display your brand to everyone who walks through your doors. Many of my clients start with a simple paper or laminated signage, or inexpensive decals that can be placed on the walls. I recommend you consider putting up simple yet beautiful posters that can be displayed at the water cooler and next to printing stations in your office space. It can even be as simple as a poster on the refrigerator in the break room.

Depending on the size of the space, you can decide how much of your Brand Trifecta is displayed. Start by putting your Tagline in prominent places, such as on doors or in main entryways. If there is room, add your Value Proposition Statement. Areas where employees frequent may warrant that the entire Brand Trifecta is displayed to more readily remember the brand and make it their own.

Finally, if you want to invest the time and money, then take it a step further with more sophisticated updates, such as murals, 3D art, and other types of more robust signage. I recommend keeping it simple to start and focus on displaying your Brand Trifecta in the more frequented areas.

Swag and Giveaway Items

If you provide marketing promotional materials to your employees, customers, and partners, then be sure to update them with your revised brand messaging. As most of these items do not allow for a lot of copy and have a limited character count for specific layouts, I recommend you focus on implementing your Tagline. Should a particular item warrant it, and should it allow for more space to add text, then consider adding your Value Proposition Statement. A good example would be on the inside cover of journals or padfolios. However, since the purpose of the swag is to provide something of value, don't inundate the receiver of the gift with too much content. Let the promotional item do the talking first, and then allow your brand to do the talking second.

Event Signage and Booth Materials

If you run events or attend trade shows, you will have numerous pieces of branded materials, such as tablecloths, banners, posters, and other items. Don't forget to update these materials with your new Brand Trifecta. Like promotional items, use your judgment on whether you include more than your Tagline, based on the amount of available space. Tablecloths and skirting can stay simple with a logo and your new Tagline. Banners and larger signage have room for your Tagline and Value Proposition Statement. If you have a larger display or booth set-up, consider adding your Differentiator Statements. Your presence at an event should be a living and breathing representation of your brand. So, don't skimp on including your Brand Trifecta so that people walking by get an immediate grasp of what you do, how you can solve their problem, and how you're different. Your Brand Trifecta will be the difference in helping you stand out from the crowd around you.

Job Descriptions

Whether you plan to hire in the immediate future or not, you will want to go back to all documented job descriptions and update them to include your new Tagline. Just as with updating company letterhead, whether you decide to insert it into the header or footer of your document is up to you. Be sure that any and all written job descriptions are updated to reflect your revised branding.

Employee Handbooks and Onboarding Materials

If there were ever a place to ensure your Brand Trifecta was alive and well, it would be within your employee handbooks and onboarding materials. Your employees are your biggest brand advocates, so it makes sense that your HR-related materials should outline your Brand Trifecta. You would want an employee to know your vision statement, mission statement, and brand values, so you should want that person to understand what you do, how you can solve your customers' problems, and how you are different from the competition.

Learning Management Systems

I firmly believe that you don't need to overcomplicate the integration of your Brand Trifecta into an LMS System. However, at a baseline, I would recommend if you have a key landing page or dashboard that employees view on a regular basis, and if you have space, incorporate your Brand Trifecta. If you are limited on character count or layout, stick with adding your Tagline to the page's headers or footers or on the primary dashboard pages. You can also integrate your entire Brand Trifecta into any other HR- related documents or learning modules in the system. The main goal is to ensure employees see your branding when they enter the system so that it is a consistent reminder of who you say you are.

Intranet or SharePoint Platforms

Just as with Learning Management Systems, intranets and SharePoint platforms do not need to be over complicated in implementing your branding. At a minimum, include your Tagline on key landing pages, dashboards, and in the headers or footers. If you have done the work of updating all your materials to your Brand Trifecta, no matter where they live, your employees can access the latest versions that best reflect your branding.

Partner or Customer Web Portals

If your customers and partners see it and use it, it should be updated. This goes for any secure portals or systems to log in to access key information. Clearly, these digital systems serve specific purposes, so I would not suggest that you try to overhaul content on key landing pages with your entire Brand Trifecta. At a minimum, include your new Tagline in the headers or footers on all web pages. However, suppose there is a particular place where you do outline company information, such as bios on the team, vision statement, and mission statement, then I recommend incorporating your Brand Trifecta into that location. Otherwise, allow your portal to be what it is, while keeping the branding updated yet minimal with the incorporation of your Tagline.

Final Thoughts on Implementing the Brand

Depending on your organization's unique needs and goals, you may have more areas where you need to implement your Brand Trifecta, or you may have less. You may have additional slide decks, workshop materials, or other digital and printed content that may need to be updated to incorporate your revised branding. Be sure to take the time and note other digital and printed documents, tools, and spaces across your organization that you may need to update. Remember, regardless of whether you implement some or all the items on this brand implementation list, try to stick with the rule of thumb—if you would update it because your company colors or logo have changed, update it because your brand message has changed.

Stay persistent, consistent, and timely in implementing your brand. Get it done quickly. Don't allow your brand to live in a box. Show it. Speak it. Live it. You will create a path of least resistance to revenue for your organization by leveraging a brand that creates conversations that convert.

ENDNOTES

The other day I watched Little Women with my daughter. She was enthralled and out of all the characters in the movie, she loved Jo March the best. I asked her why.

She looked up, smiled, and said, "Because, mom. She is happy and free. I want to be just like her."

There have been very few times that I have been rendered speechless, and this was one of them.

My vivacious child of only seven years old somehow understood the heart of the matter more than I ever have. Jo's story is about more than muting the megaphone. It is about freedom. It's about joy. It's about living one's life on brand.

I wake up each day with a humble recognition that my daughter is watching. I pray she sees more than a business owner, a brand expert, or even a mother and wife. I hope that she sees glimpses of the glorious Jo March when she sees me. I hope she sees Jo March within herself.

My daughter, may you not just live. May you thrive.

ABOUT THE AUTHOR

An "accidental brand strategist" who originally intended to pursue a Ph.D. in Anthropology, Kate DiLeo discovered the power of branding during her first sales job. In the pursuit of making quota, Kate realized she needed to cut through the noise with a message that would compel prospects to want to have a conversation. It was that, or she was out of a job.

Kate overcame, honed her craft, and went on to successfully manage millions in pipeline by throwing out the long monologue sales scripts and unsubscribing leads from complex story-based marketing campaigns. Instead, she delivered a simple pitch that invited prospects to engage in a compelling conversation by sharing what she did, how she could solve their problem, and how she differed from the competition.

That pitch, which Kate calls, The Brand Trifecta, is rooted in her firm belief that brand is the path of least resistance to revenue. The ability to clearly articulate these three points offers the prospect all the information they need to opt-in and say, "Now that's interesting. I want to have a conversation." Throughout her career in both agency and corporate settings, she pursued her branding side hustle until 2019, when she turned it into her full-time business.

Kate is also a #1 international bestselling author and she is honored to have worked with more than 300 brands across 25+ sectors. She is passionate about partnering with founder-led organizations that desire to craft an authentic, purpose-driven message to effectively get more prospects to the table, more users who click, and more customers who buy.

ACKNOWLEDGEMENTS

I would like to express deep-in-my-bones gratitude to the following:

My God, from whom my very being comes and my very breath flows. I will spend the rest of my life trying to get the words right to tell You what I fully mean. For now, I will simply say thank You for loving me and giving me life.

My dear husband—you are my person. Thank you for choosing me, choosing us, and choosing our family each day. There is nothing more precious, my sweet man, than holding your hand as we walk this road of life.

My remarkable children (birth child and bonus children alike)— you are my joy, my peace, my strength, and my song. I am so proud of the confident, brave, kind, smart, and strong humans you are. Thank you for waking me up each morning and reminding me that the role of "Mama" trumps "CEO" every day.

My wonderful parents and sister—you are the embodiment of faithfulness. Thank you for always being there, loving me unconditionally, and putting up with my crazy shenanigans over the years. Dad's mantra has certainly come true: A family that prays, eats, and laughs together surely sticks together.

B. and V.—you have always seen me as more than my words and deeds, but as the whole of who I am becoming in God's grace. Thank you for being women who truly walk the walk, and thank you for standing with me as I seek to live my most faithful and courageous life.

The "Founding Fathers"—you know who you are, and you are family. Thank you for being the most incredible group of impact- focused entrepreneurs with whom I could ever hope to do business and life. I am better and braver because of each of you.

Carolyn Flower of Oxygen Publishing—you are simply the best. This book would not exist without your belief, support, and expertise. Thank you for championing the author in me. The best is surely yet to come, my friend, as it has already been written in firm assurance.

And finally, The Naysayers—you said I was too big, too bold, and too much. You were right. I am too big, too bold, and too much for the parameters and perceptions by which the world tries to define me. Thank you for igniting an unquenchable fire within me to forever treasure the remarkability of who I am. Your judgment has led to my own acceptance. What a gift it is to no longer live my life on your terms, but my own.

Are you ready to build a brand that wins
more work in only 4 - 6 weeks?

———✦———

Learn more:
www.BrandTrifecta.com

www.KateDiLeo.com

KATE DILEO

Made in the USA
Middletown, DE
28 October 2023